# CREATION

## THE AMAZING STORY OF A SMALL BLUE PLANET

# WALK

BRIAN GROGAN SJ

First published in 2020 by Messenger Publications

ISBN: 978 1 788121 200

Scripture quotations are from several versions, including the New
Revised Standard Version which is used by permission.
All rights reserved worldwide.

Designed by Messenger Publications Design Department
Typeset in Albertina, Amelia, Avenir Next Condensed
Printed by Hussar Books

Messenger Publications,
37 Lower Place, Dublin D02 E5V0, Ireland
www.messenger.ie

## Acknowledgements

Thanks to Phyllis Brady, Catherine Brennan,
Neal Carlin, Paul Grogan, Anne Lyons,
and the Knock Faith Renewal Council
for support and inspiration.

# TABLE OF CONTENTS

## PART ONE
## THE NEW STORY OF CREATION ~ 10

## PART TWO
## THE CREATION WALK ~ 26

# PART THREE
# WHAT HOPE FOR
# A SMALL BLUE PLANET? ~ 94

# PART ONE

# THE NEW STORY OF CREATION

# 1: The New Cosmology

Welcome to a new world! Only within the last 100 years did astrophysicists discover that our seemingly steady universe is in fact expanding. This discovery enabled them to pinpoint the moment when the universe must have begun, some 13.8 billion years ago. Only in 1969 did photos from Apollo 8 first reveal to our amazed eyes the whole Earth in its extraordinary and delicate beauty, and so we began to live in a imaginatively richer world. Our remote ancestors had sat around campfires 100,000 years ago and with few resources tried to puzzle out where they were, where they had originated from and the meaning of their existence. Now we, their descendants, suddenly have access to a treasury of data which enables us to travel the long Creation Walk and be astonished at the improbable twists and turns that have brought us to the present. The tale told here in an arbitrary thirty stages is being continuously updated and expanded by science, for we are still only on the edge of the ocean of the unknown.

Our topic is the new cosmology (Greek: *cosmos* = world order, *logos* = knowledge), which is universally accessible today. It is an area of knowledge bordered by deep mystery. But mystery attracts us. We are a species distinguished by endless curiosity, wherever it may take us, and such exploration is deeply enriching. Like our ancestors we find ourselves asking: 'Who am I?' 'What am I made for?' 'Shall I live after death?' 'Where are the dead?' 'Does it matter more to try to live well within the mystery of life rather than try to sort out these profound questions?'

Our short life-spans seem to be mysteries to be lived within a greater mystery. When your wonder is aroused about anything, you can see this as mystery gently opening a door: by stepping through you enter a richer world and find traces of what is strangely satisfying.

Rachel Carson, author of *Silent Spring,* which sparked our current concern for the environment, wrote: 'If I had influence with the good fairy who is supposed to preside over the christening of all children, I should ask that her gift to each child be a sense of wonder so indestructible that it would last throughout life'. So wherever you are on life's journey, you are in a good place to explore the Story of Creation: just allow it to unfold and lead you on. A breathtaking revelation of the wonder and majesty of things awaits you through the new cosmology, even if intellectual honesty may require you to hold off from the religious formulations that accompany the stages outlined here. Such formulations are intended as humble signposts to the Great Mystery underlying all science and religion.

Some of our early ancestors believed that the Earth was flat with the sky above it; others held that Earth sat firmly in the sea on the back of a giant turtle. Then one day 2,600 years ago a thoughtful Greek named Anaximander realised that the sky envelops the Earth on *all* sides; he also pictured Earth as a great stone sphere, hanging in the centre of the universe, with the heavenly bodies revolving around it. Only 500 years ago Copernicus found scientific proof that in fact Earth revolves around the sun, and less than a century ago the Hubble telescope revealed that our galaxy, the Milky Way, is only one of billions of galaxies, and that the universe is constantly expanding. Even since I began writing this booklet, astrophysicists and scientists have discovered more and more about the extraordinary weave of the reality around us.

Such is the new cosmology described in these pages. I feel like the farmer in the Zen story who looked up from his evening toil, saw the moon and excitedly pointed at it with a carrot so others might admire what he saw. So don't get fixated on the carrot – my text – but on the cosmos itself. Put on your mystery boots, cancel your membership of the Flat Earth Society and step out with surprise into a whole new way of seeing the world. If you are a believer you will meet God in new and unexpected ways, and be lost in awe and wonder at how each thing, simply by being in existence, gives God praise. The phrase 'Glory be to God!' takes on a new depth of meaning, and you become a cantor of the beauty of the cosmos.

# 2: SCIENCE AND SCRIPTURE

Science and Scripture collaborate seamlessly to tell this new story of Creation: these distinct domains of knowledge enrich each other. The theological insights underpinning the Scriptures remain firm as the body of scientific truth expands in endlessly surprising ways: that God creates, blesses and provides for everything that exists, that male and female are made in God's image and likeness, that God desires our friendship, that we are related by origin to the other species and owe them respect and care and that divine love is working steadily to irradiate all Creation with divinity and glory. Science opens curtains to reveal precious insights on *how* God orchestrates the mystery that we call Creation.

St John Paul II in 1992 apologised for the condemnation of Galileo (1564–1642) when he wrote

> The error of the theologians of the time was to think that our understanding of the structure of the physical world was, in some way, imposed by the literal sense of Sacred Scripture'. In 1998 he noted: 'Science can purify religion from error and superstition, while religion can purify science from false absolutes. Each can draw the other into a wider world in which both can flourish.

Einstein arrived at the same conclusion:

> Through my scientific work I have come to believe

more and more strongly that the physical universe is put together with an ingenuity so astonishing that I cannot accept it merely as a brute fact. There must be a deeper level of explanation: whether one wishes to call that deeper level 'God' is a matter of taste and definition.

Richard Dawkins, author of *The God Delusion*, surprisingly accepts that he is 'religious' in the following meaning of that word:

To sense that behind anything that can be experienced there is a something that our mind cannot grasp, and whose beauty and sublimity reaches us only indirectly and as a feeble reflection – this is religiousness. In this sense I am religious.

Carlo Rovelli, theoretical physicist and author of *Reality is Not What It Seems,* creates an awesome picture of the reality within which we find ourselves:

We are made up of the same atoms and the same light signals as are exchanged between pine trees in the mountains and stars in the galaxies. We live in a colorful and amazing world where a universe explodes into being, space collapses into bottomless holes, time slows near a planet, and the unbounded extensions of inter-stellar space ripple and sway like the surface of the sea. Here, on the edge of what we know, in contact with the ocean of the unknown, shines the mystery and the beauty of the world. And it's breathtaking.

# 3: Finding God in Creation

As we walk the long time-line of Creation we find that the truths of Sacred Scripture are interwoven with those of contemporary science to enrich our understanding of our Common Home. God is author both of the book of Scriptures and the book of Nature. If you find God in small things you will be more able to find God on the macro-level. A feather, a leaf, a drop of water, a single breath – any tiny and passing thing can open a window onto the divine. The eighteenth-century botanist Linnaeus noted that 'Nature is most to be marveled at in the smallest of creatures'. Pope Francis's landmark encyclical on the environment, *Laudato Si'*, 2015, says that Nature is 'a continuing revelation of the divine' (LS, 85). When you accept this fact the everyday world around you is transfigured and life becomes a song of gratitude.

But *Laudato Si'* carries a challenge too:

> If we approach nature without openness to awe and wonder, if we no longer speak the language of fraternity in our relationship with the world, our attitude will be that of ruthless exploiters… But if we feel intimately united with all that exists, then care will well up spontaneously in us (LS, 11).

For the Passionist priest Thomas Berry, co-author with Brian Swimme of the groundbreaking book, *The Universe Story*, the key mission of modern education is to reveal the true importance of the Creation Story for all our earthly affairs. Our role, he argues, is *to create* its next phase. Once you become aware of how delicately balanced Nature is, you find yourself falling in love with it. Then you can work and pray for the protection of its beauty. When Jesus prays, '*May they all be one*' he is asking for the growth of universal harmony between the divine, humankind and all Creation.

We humans, though late arrivals on Planet Earth, are destroying it. We must undergo a painful conversion and learn to live in harmony and communion with all the species that preceded us and made our world so beautiful. Through us the universe can celebrate itself in a unique mode of conscious self-awareness. Our story is numinous, sacred and revelatory. It is both our personal and our community story because it took nothing less than the collaboration of the universe to bring humans into being!

Carl Sagan, an astrophysicist with a gift for communication, humorously reminds us that to make an apple pie from scratch, you'd need a whole universe! Is this true? Well, think of your kitchen, its cement and wood, its lighting, its gadgets, especially the cooker – already you have involved the vast world of technology. Then consider the apples, flour, sugar and water – behind them is the history of agriculture, which in turn involves clay, metals, water, heat and atmosphere. Add in electricity and energy for the cooking. And of course you need Earth to work on, not to mention yourself as cook, for you are not self-made but owe your origin to stardust. Everything is indeed interconnected: the making of an apple pie is a collaborative and global event! Creation is a seamless weave of which our lives are meant to be a part. We are to be in tune with the symphony of things, singers in the chorus rather than hecklers and disrupters.

We are invited to grow in appreciation of our planet, which provides us with marvelous human beings, with an abundance of food to nourish us, with exquisite beauty of form and colour, with delicate fragrances and with exciting challenges that evoke skill, imagination, joy and collaboration. Only this new consciousness can convert us from a devastating exploitation of Earth into a supportive and respectful presence to one another and to all our neighbouring species and natural surroundings. This is what eco-conversion entails: it is not for Christians only but for everyone; it has always been central, for example, to Buddhists, and from their wisdom we can learn a great deal.

# 4: A LOVING GAZE

How can we meet the challenge to eco-conversion? For a moment sit back and ask yourself, '*What is precious to me?*' Think of something or someone that perhaps means a lot to you, and which if it were endangered you would rush to save: a baby, a friend, a love-letter, an heirloom, a home, a tree, a new car, a work of art. If it were injured, trashed or destroyed, how would you feel?

Now consider that Creation, down to its least speck, is precious to God. Ask God, '*Why do you risk entrusting this treasure to us humans?*' Must God not feel dismayed when we destroy the forests, ravage the earth, pollute the oceans and treat billions of tons of Creation as trash? Do we bring grief to God, as to an artist who sees their handiwork being destroyed? We are told that we can grieve the Holy Spirit (Eph 4:30), and we know that Jesus wept over Jerusalem. The real God is a God of infinite care, whose Creation is a precious gift to be treasured and tended, and Earth is Common Home not only to us but to God as well, since Jesus pitched his tent among us. Ours is to be a civilisation of care.

*Laudato Si'* states that everything we see is a letter in the magnificent Book of Creation. It is for us to connect up the letters and to realise that God is manifested in all that exists. God, it has been said, is materialised in a robin, a sunset, a stone, a leaf. So close is God that everything is, so to speak, a caress of God, a revelation of the divine. 'Everything' includes human constructions, as the Pope notes:

> Technology, when well directed, can produce important means of improving the quality of human life, from useful domestic appliances to great transportation systems, bridges, buildings and public spaces. It can also produce art and enable men and women immersed in the material world to leap into the world of beauty. Who can deny the beauty of an aircraft or a skyscraper? (LS, 103).

The simplest thing discloses a new aspect of God's beauty, originality, imaginativeness. To see things thus is to be enveloped in the wonderful mystery of the Beyond, and helps us to recover the contemplative capacity of our childhood when everything was full of wonder, before we named, objectified and categorised it. The loving gaze sees things in terms of their beauty prior to their usefulness or function.

A poet tells of a father and his little son watching a cart go up the street. 'That's Murphy's cart' says the father, and turns away, but the child is captivated by the horse – its beauty and strength, its magnificence, its sheer being. The contemplative stance can revive such moments in us, and restore us to an enchanting world. Poets have this gift, and mystics too, but we can share what they see: the blind in the Gospels who are healed can include us too. As the poet William Blake puts it: 'If the doors of our perception were cleansed, everything would appear as it is, infinite'. We can cultivate this deeper perception.

An old teacher used to say, '*Talk to the grass, children!*' So consider a simple leaf: gaze on and admire it. Learn about it: its arteries and veins – complex pipelines that transport water, carbon and nutrients to where they are needed; note its capacity to transform sunlight and water into food and energy for its parent plant. Learn how twig and leaf enrich each other.

Now with a touch of imagination take a step further: just as people talk to their pets and plants, invite the leaf to tell its history. After all, what makes childhood books like *The Wind in the Willows* so captivating is the personalising of Rat and Mole: they are not portrayed as objects but as having histories and emotions like ourselves. The Psalmist tells the hills to sing for joy and clap their hands, and Pope Francis speaks of each creature singing the hymn of its existence. God, he says, is trying to teach us even through a leaf. To contemplate is to hear a message, it is to listen to a silent voice (LS, 85). So imagine the leaf telling its story: it can't use words, so be its spokesperson. This breaks downs the duality of subject and object: even a dead leaf gains significance when you ask it about its origins, its life, its joys and griefs, its dying, its future. Let it in turn speak to you of your own life, and what you share in common with it. Gradually you will find yourself linked in mysteriously with the other leaves of the world.

Each thing has levels of meaning, depending on the spectator. A field means one thing to the farmer but something else to the developer: a neighbour may well covet it, but the elder son sees it as his inheritance. The cows and the myriad of species that live in it see it as home. And the contemplative tries to see it simply as it is: as gift, as awesome, as rich mystery, as offering a simple path to the divine. Irish poet Patrick Kavanagh found God in a cut-away bog, and saw people 'as small as they really were, which meant as great as God had made them'.

We may be only mini-mystics with L-plates on our backs, but we can touch into the mystery of things at every turn, and a deeper way of seeing can open out for us. We can consciously connect here and now to the Great Mystery which pulsates through all things. As Thomas Merton says, the gates of heaven are everywhere. Just as particle physicists spend their lives exploring the micro-levels of reality, every scrap that exists around us offers the raw material for prayer.

# 5: CLIMATE GRIEF AND CHRISTIAN HOPE

As the Sixth Mass Extinction becomes daily more real, the world goes on its customary way, though climate grief and despair are beginning to haunt many people. Have we indeed passed the tipping point for our planet? Scientific predictions are ominous: Wallace-Wells begins his epoch-defining book, *The Uninhabitable Earth*, as follows: 'It is worse, much worse than you think'. Are we like the disciples at the Last Supper, eating, drinking and arguing, perhaps with a dim sense that all is not well but totally unaware of what's around the corner?

On what grounds, if any, can we hope that the current sickness of Earth can be reversed?

When I speak of hope I mean a hope that is firmly grounded in God's goodness, power and wisdom, and which makes us open to do what God wants of us. The simple divine command, 'Go!' rings out across the Scriptures when things are at their lowest, and if obeyed, the impossible happens and disaster is averted. So with Abraham (Gen 12:1), with Gideon (Judg 6:14) with Jeremiah (Jer 1:7), with Moses (Ex 3:16 etc) and many others. When Moses protests his unsuitability – '*Who am I to go to Pharaoh?*'– God clarifies where the needed power lies: '*Who gives speech to mortals, who makes them mute or deaf, seeing or blind? Is it not I, the Lord? Now go, and I will be with you and teach you what you are to speak*' (Ex 4:13). Our task is to trust desperately, to stay close to God and to do what God asks. Such hope unlocks energy and creativity.

So as you walk with Creation with this book in hand, notice that each successive creative step is unpredictable before it happens: it is orchestrated by the Author of reality, often out of near disaster. '*I am about to do a new thing. My thoughts are not your thoughts, nor are your ways my ways, says the Lord*' (Isa 43:19; 55:8). This promise gives no grounds for a fatalistic passivity but it does offer a reason for trusting in the possibility of further divine intervention whereby ultimately all will be made well. Francis Thompson's closing words in 'The Hound of Heaven' might be impossibly true:

> All which thy child's mistake
> Fancies as lost, I have stored for thee at home.
> Rise, clasp My hand and come!

We will pick up this theme of Christian hope in part three, but in the meantime Jeremiah's image of the potter may help us to focus on our Creator God who can always do what is best.

*I went down to the potter's house, and there he was, working at his wheel. The vessel he was making was spoiled in his hand, so he reworked it into another vessel, as seemed good to him. Then the word of the Lord came to me: 'Can I not do with you just as this potter has done? Just as the clay in the potter's hand, so are you in my hand.'*

(Jer 18:3–6)

*Some people, in order to discover God, read books.*
*But there exists already a great book,*
*the very appearance of created things.*
*Look above you!*
*Read it!*
*God, whom you want to discover,*
*never wrote that book with ink.*
*Instead he set before your eyes*
*the things that he made.*
*Can you ask for a louder voice than that?*
*Why, heaven and earth shout to you: 'God made me!'*

St Augustine, 354–430, *The City of God*, Book XVI

# PART TWO

# THE CREATION WALK

# MAKING THE MOST OF THE CREATION WALK

Since the chronology of the cosmos was established some forty years ago, Cosmic or Universe Walks have been designed indoors and outdoors to help us to appreciate with all our senses the unfolding story of Creation. Such Walks follow the unfolding of the Cosmos from its origin to the present. Significant changes and unexpected emergences are highlighted.

If you can access an outdoor Creation Walk, give a generous amount of time to completing it. As I write, such a Walk is in preparation on the beautiful campus of Knock Shrine, Co. Mayo, Ireland. It's worth the journey! School groups and others can engage interactively with the Walk by reading this booklet first and then creatively acting out some of its stages. But even by browsing leisurely over these pages at home, you can walk slowly through the doors of Time, and note what God reveals at each period of cosmic history. The whole Creation is '*groaning*' to tell us its story (Rom 8:22). The Walk becomes a prayer as you watch the scroll of reality unfolding.

Stop at each halting-sign and spend a little time imagining the event indicated. Try to enter its mystery with surprise, awe and wonder. As you move along I invite you to say *'Wow! What happened next?'* Be amazed at the totally unexpected twists by which the web of life becomes ever more diverse yet also more interconnected.

Pray as you go for the grace to connect with all that is being revealed to you. At the end you know better the world in which you live, and you have a deeper sense of the awesome imagination of its Creator. You also know more about the constituents and processes that have produced your own self, because this is your story. You were present – in an embryonic way – from the beginning of the emergence of the universe. How does it feel to know that your family tree extends back not just a number of generations, but 13.8 billion years? This insight on your remarkable genealogy can bring you to a new sense of relatedness to the other members of the human race, past and present, and to a new compassion for all other species with which you share Planet Earth.

Finally, as you end the Walk, imagine all the earth's species gathered in harmony around the Table of Creation, enjoying the glorious mystery of each other. Suddenly the fellowship is shattered as a greedy hand swoops down and begins to destroy one species after another. See the fear and dismay of a small bird, or a snail, or a wild animal, or a rare flower, as it whispers to you, *'Can we depend on you to do what you can to save us?'*

How do you respond? This is what eco-conversion is about …

# Step 1
# The Birth
# of the Cosmos

## 13,800,000,000 years ago

In 1650 Archbishop Ussher of Armagh pronounced that God began the week-long work of Creation at 6 pm on the evening of Saturday 22 October 4004 BC. With the scientific data now to hand we know that our universe in fact flared into existence some 13.8 billion years ago: we call that moment the Big Bang. Time, space and energy began to exist. All that would ever come to be has developed from the processes of hydrogen and helium formation that began then and still continue. The universe expanded and cooled rapidly. Energy condensed into matter.

As the author of *Once Upon a Universe* puts it: 'We now know that the sacred community of the universe is a single interconnected web of life emanating from the creative energy of God. Before the beginning there was silence. No time, no space … nothing … only Spirit. Suddenly everything burst forth from a single point – energy erupting with the brilliance of a trillion stars and the combined speed of a million hurricanes. This fireball flared forth in every direction, creating time and space. All the matter that exists now was present then in embryonic form. Every particle in the universe is at source connected to all others.'

Nancy Sylvester continues: 'We humans have emerged from stardust. We were nourished in the oceans but risked coming onto land. There we stood tall, breathed in air, and learnt to till the soil for food. We have fallen in love, written poetry, sung songs, created stories about our origins, performed rituals, prayed to our deities and wished well to the dead. Now as an Earth community we explore Creation from its tiniest to its cosmic manifestations to learn how to live with the reverence our ancestors had for our Common Home.'

*'In the beginning*
*God created the heavens*
*and the earth'.*
(Gen 1:1)

## 'WOW! WHAT HAPPENED NEXT?'

# STEP 2
# GALAXIES

## 12,800,000,000 years ago

Across the Universe, stars just like our sun made of hydrogen and helium began to cluster together in their billions forming what we call galaxies: the Milky Way, to which we belong, is our nearest example. As larger stars in their death throes exploded – supernovas – they created in their wombs the heavier elements such as carbon, calcium, iron. These provided the fundamental suite of constituents for life as we know it to emerge.

The universe is permeated with an extraordinary power of creativity. On one end of the spectrum is the whale, on the other the fairy-fly, the smallest insect ever observed. This little being has an average body length of just 0.139mm, almost as thin as a strand of hair. Yet its body consists of 1,690,000,000,000 atoms.

### Clouds of Galaxies

Although we used to think that our Earth had a privileged place at the centre of the Universe, we now know that our solar system is only one among a vast number of others. Planet Earth, the tiny cosmic gem entrusted to human care, is an infinitesimal speck in the corner of our galaxy, which is a vast cloud of one hundred billion stars. And there are more shocks: the nebulae (*nebula* = cloud), which we can see between the stars are in fact clouds of galaxies, each one containing a hundred billion suns similar to ours. The majority of these suns are orbited by planets. So there are in the universe thousands of billions of billions of billions of planets such as Earth.

We are invited to pay amazed attention both to the size of the universe and to God who looks after our Common Home so carefully. We are being drawn forward by the Author of all Cosmic Mystery who is manifested in created things and who leaves a divine signature on all that exists. The 'Beyond' beckons us through scientific discoveries that steadily unveil more and more of the mystery in which we are immersed.

> *'The heavens are telling the glory of God,*
> *and the firmament shows forth*
> *the work of God's hands'.*
> (Ps 19:1)

# 'WOW! WHAT HAPPENED NEXT?'

# Step 3
# Molecules

## 11,800,000,000 Years Ago

Within interstellar dust the chemical gifts of the supernovas were nurtured into simple organic molecules, vital components for the later emergence of life.

### Particles and Molecules

A molecule (*moles* = mass, *cula* = small) is a particle made up of two or more atoms, so molecules are chemically-bound groupings of elemental atoms derived from stellar dust. A small set of elementary particles is used in Nature's recipes with astonishingly varied results. Each speck of my chair is ultimately made up of small particles connected together in whatever form Nature assigns them. So the hidden make-up of our world has an attractive simplicity about it – particles and electro-magnetic fields, all busy about their business!

Electro-magnetic fields? Imagine the attracting power of magnets, and the power of electricity: electro-magnetic fields emit waves that make the particles around them dance. When the world of atoms and sub-atomic particles is opened up, we find that is a continuous, restless swarming cloud of particles that vibrate and also fluctuate between existence and non-existence. The particles are like wavelets on a seemingly placid lake. No wave is alone; a calm lake is a rapid dance of water molecules, which combine to give us $H_2O$. Heat makes atoms and molecules move around more quickly, in cold substances they move more slowly.

The components of what we see are atoms: each atom is a nucleus surrounded by electrons, and each nucleus contains protons and neutrons which in turn are made up of even smaller particles called 'quarks' (from Joyce's *Finnegans Wake*), while the force that holds quarks inside protons and neutrons is happily called a 'gluon'. We are caught up in their dance, and bonded with every other particle in the universe. Ongoing and unpredictable change characterises the micro-world.

Think now about all the particles you ate for breakfast! Ask yourself, 'Am I composed of molecules and atoms? And did I originate – literally – in stardust?' If you reflect back far enough, let's say 11.8 billion years – the answer to both questions is yes!

*'O the depth of the riches and wisdom and knowledge of God! How unsearchable are God's judgements and ways!'*
(Rom 11:33)

# 'WOW! WHAT HAPPENED NEXT?'

# STEP 4
# SUN AND EARTH

## 4,600,000,000 years ago

It took nine billion years after the Big Bang for our solar system and Earth to emerge. An old star, our 'grandmother' star, exploded and the enormous volume of released matter became consolidated into our Sun and the members of our solar system. Here begins the story of Planet Earth, which by now is some 4.6 billion years old. It will last for several billion years more, and it is now in a mid-life crisis!

*Our Moving Cosmos*
How stable is Earth, given that in the cosmos everything is moving fast? The facts are as follows: galaxies are moving away from one another, the Sun moves around our Milky Way galaxy in a huge orbit at 483,000 miles per hour, Earth is anchored to the Sun by gravity and is travelling at 19 miles per second or 67,000 miles per hour. As if that were not enough to make us dizzy, the Earth spins on its own axis at 1000

miles per hour. Happily the pull of Earth's gravity holds us in place, so we are not flung into space.

When the first astronauts looked back at the Earth they called it the 'Blue Planet': this is no surprise since 70% of Earth is covered with oceans. The remaining 30% is solid ground above sea level. Earth is mostly iron (32%), oxygen (30%), silicon (15%) and magnesium (14%). Only 3% of the water is fresh: 2% is frozen in ice sheets and glaciers, so less than 1% of the world's fresh water is found in lakes, rivers and underground. Each winter a trillion trillion snow crystals fall from the sky. Sadly, in some coal-burning areas, snow now falls as black.

Earth was born out of massive explosions and collisions. It is beautiful, fragile and friendly to us, and we are asked to respect its delicacy, its subtle balances and its steady care of us.

'O LORD, THE HEAVENS ARE YOURS,
THE EARTH ALSO IS YOURS; THE WORLD
AND ALL THAT IS IN IT'.
(Ps 89:11)

# 'WOW! WHAT HAPPENED NEXT?'

# STEP 5
# THE MOON

## 4,300,000,000 years ago

While still a fluid molten ball, Earth may have been impacted by a Mars-sized planet that caused some of its outer layers to splash out and solidify into our Moon. That would answer the question of why so much of the Moon's makeup is similar to that of Earth.

The Moon's distance from Earth is 239,000 miles. It is one quarter of the diameter of Earth, which it orbits every 29.5 days. Travel time to the Moon by Apollo 11 is three days, or by car 135 days at 70 miles per hour!

*Our Moon*
On 21 July 1969, Niall Armstrong became the first person to set foot on the Moon, 'a giant step for humankind'. His companion, Edwin Aldwin, a devout Presbyterian, took communion on the Moon's surface, read from Scripture and invited those watching from Earth to give thanks, each in their own way. Every day on Earth this thanksgiving takes place in the Eucharist that blesses the

goodness of God, who is addressed as 'Lord God of all creation'.

Earth's relationship with the Sun and Moon choreographs its exquisite dance of life. Tides are caused by the complex interaction of the gravity of Sun, Earth and Moon on Earth's water. Poets rhapsodise about the Moon and Francis of Assisi would ring the Church bells to get the townsfolk out to admire her.

Earth is the only planet in our solar system with an atmosphere that can sustain life. Its blanket of gases not only contains the air that we breathe but also protects us from the heat and radiation emanating from the sun. The atmosphere warms the planet by day, cools it at night and is mainly composed of nitrogen and oxygen. Most of the atmosphere is within 10 miles of the Earth's surface.

*'I look at your heavens, the work*
*of your hands,*
*the moon and the stars that*
*you have established'.*
(Ps 8:3)

# 'WOW! WHAT HAPPENED NEXT?'

# STEP 6
# WATER AND EARTH

## 4,100,000,000 years ago

Earth formed its atmosphere as it slowly cooled. Steam condensed above the Earth and rain and weather cycles began. Torrential rains fell: rivers ran over the land and merged to become oceans, which are salty because of mineral deposits washed down from land. Clouds began to cocoon the Earth, and in their changing beauty can be called God's calligraphy or God's palette.

*Earth*
What is the composition of Planet Earth, which is home to countless species of plants and animals besides ourselves?

It may seem to us that Earth is one big solid rock, but in fact it is layered like an onion. The four main layers are the Outer Crust, Mantle, Outer Core, and Inner Core.

*The Outer Crust*, on which every living thing exists, is made of clay and rock which varies from 5–70km thick. At its weak spots volcanoes emerge.

*The Mantle* is also made up of rocks and is some 3000km thick. The tectonic plates are a combination of the Crust and the Mantle. They move a couple of inches a year, and when they touch, earthquakes and tsunamis occur.

*Earth's Outer Core* is inside the Mantle and is made up of iron and nickel: it is so hot (4500+ °C) that the metals are in liquid form. This Outer Core creates a magnetic field in space, a barrier that shields us from the sun's damaging solar winds.

*Earth's Inner Core* is also made up of iron and nickel, but is so deep within the earth and under so much pressure that, even though it is so hot, it is solid. The Inner Core at over 5000 °C is as hot as the surface of the sun.

Earth is 4.6 billion years old: after some 2 billion years an increased energy output from the Sun will begin to boil our oceans, and while Earth will survive it will be no more than an exhausted and lifeless planet.

*'God said, "Let the waters under the sky be gathered together into one place, and let the dry land appear". And it was so. God called the dry land Earth, and the waters God called Seas.'*

(Gen 1:9–10)

# 'WOW! WHAT HAPPENED NEXT?'

# STEP 7
# THE FIRST CELLS

## 4,000,000,000 years ago

Within the newly formed oceans a rich variety of chemicals gathered together in the form of primitive bacteria-like organisms. Earth awoke into life.

### Bacteria

What are bacteria? All organisms are made of 'cells', tiny bags of living matter that come in different shapes and sizes. The living things with which we are most familiar consist of multitudes of cells, many of which have developed in specialised forms that make particular organs – bones, roots, lungs, flower petals. But by far the most numerous forms of life are micro-organisms, each of which is made up of just a single cell. Bacteria are the best known group, and they are found everywhere on Earth. The shape of the 'Tree of Life' suggests that bacteria-like unicellular organisms were the first life-forms, and that all of life's subsequent diversity evolved from these common ancestors. In other words, all living things – including you and me – are ultimately descended from humble bacteria-like organisms, whose fossils date back 3.5 billion years.

## *DNA*

A single human cell contains enough DNA molecules to stretch to about 2 meters if it were not tightly coiled. Human DNA is divided into 46 molecules (one long DNA molecule for each chromosome). Since the human body consists of a vast number of cells the total length of DNA in a single person would stretch to the sun and back about 50 times. DNA is like a computer software program that provides the recipe information to manufacture various proteins which are the fundamental building blocks of all cell-types. The complete set of genetic material in a cell (the genome [gene + chromosome]) carries the story of our evolution, and connects us with bacteria, butterflies and barracuda: the great chain of being is linked through DNA.

Whence the genetic code? Scientists spend their days trying to build even a single living cell, while we have some 86 billion cells in our brain, and 30 trillion in our body! The Royal Society's Evolution Prize, worth 10 million dollars, will go to the first person who can bridge the gap between physics and biology and create a living cell. Of course the winner must use only materials and conditions such as would have been to hand 4 billion years ago!

*'I will praise you, God, because I am fearfully and wonderfully made'.* (Ps 139:14)

# 'WOW! WHAT HAPPENED NEXT?'

# STEP 8
# PHOTOSYNTHESIS

## 3,700,000,000 years ago

Rather than just feeding off chemical compounds in the waters around them, some bacteria evolved ways to capture energy directly from the sun, thus creating new sources of food from carbon dioxide, water and simple minerals. Leaves appeared only billions of years later, but photosynthesis (*photo* = light, *synthesis* = combination) describes their extraordinary capacity to draw in the sun's energy, to transform carbon dioxide and water into carbohydrates, and so to nourish their parent plant. However, oxygen is released as a byproduct. Oxygen is a powerful element that breaks up many biological molecules, and is toxic unless an organism has specialised protective adaptations. Happily the dynamics of our little planet provided a self-correcting capacity, as we shall see below.

### Ordered Chance
A delicate balance holds the cosmos together. 'Had the supernova not exploded five billion years ago, had the

earth not maintained a certain temperature so that water would flow and life emerge, had the ozone not processed out certain levels of radiation, had the original fireball lasted just a few seconds longer or shorter than it did over 750,000 years, or maintained a temperature just one degree hotter or colder over that long period of time, we humans would not exist. We were indeed loved by the cosmos from the beginning' – Matthew Fox.

There exists in the universe a dynamic pattern whereby order emerges out of chaos. Without chaos (*chaos* = disorder, confusion), there would be no change, while without the dynamic pattern, order would not emerge. Pierre Teilhard de Chardin SJ speaks of 'blind searching' and 'ordered chance': for him the idea of 'God making things make themselves' is the most beautiful of all forms of creativity. Bernard Lonergan SJ speaks of 'a fluid stability' and 'emergent probability' that brings forth novelty and development, but also false starts and breakdowns. Earth is hospitable to life, but if the delicate order of things is ravaged, as occurs through global warming and human insensitivity, chaos ensues. Our ecological conversion is urgent. Exercises such as this Creation Walk help us to catch on to the order and rhythms of Nature and to collaborate closely with her.

*'God saw everything God had made,*
*and indeed it was very good'.*
(Gen 1:31)

# 'WOW! WHAT HAPPENED NEXT?'

# STEP 9
# A BREATHING WORLD

## 2,000,000,000 years ago

A new source of energy developed with breathing. The slow build-up of oxygen enabled some bacteria to make use of the high energy associated with the consumption of oxygen. This capacity so favored development that other bacterial species engulfed some of the oxygen-using cells that remained functional within the host species. Thus there emerged a living together of one organism within another, called symbiosis (*sym* = together, *bios* = life). Further evolution of such cells led to the segregation of DNA into the nuclear cell, the basis for the evolution of all complex life-forms.

### Life and Happiness
What is life? Ask the scientists, but they can't yet define it.

And what is *human* life about? Has it a worthwhile purpose, a satisfying meaning? Or is life simply 'a tale told by an idiot, full of sound and fury, signifying nothing', as Macbeth puts it?

The philosopher Aristotle in the fourth century BC, offers a surprising answer: '*Happiness* is the meaning and the purpose of life, the whole aim and goal of human existence.'

The Bible is also surprising. It has rightly been called 'the Book of Suffering' but this description eclipses its key message that joy, happiness, blessedness are indeed our destiny! Between them, terms such as *joy*, *blessed* and *happy* recur over 150 times in the New Testament.

St Paul can say, '*Rejoice in the Lord always! Again I say, Rejoice!*' because we are made by God and made for God, and God is pure joy, blessedness, happiness. God's joy is at the core of our DNA, so we are created to be happy. '*To be near God is my happiness*' (Ps 73:28). Happiness is revealed as intimacy with the divine.

The Holy Spirit within us indicates that divine life, joy and radiant happiness are already given to us. Jesus prays, '*May my joy remain in you and your joy be full*' (Jn 15:11). When everything is said and done, we are infinitely loved. As Pope Benedict says, 'Each of us is willed, loved, necessary!' This is our astounding destiny!

### 'I WANT YOU TO BE HAPPY, ALWAYS HAPPY IN THE LORD'.

(Phil 4:4)

# 'WOW! WHAT HAPPENED NEXT?'

# STEP 10
# MULTI-CELLED LIFE

## 1,000,000,000 years ago

The first organisms were single-celled and reproduced by simple division (cloning). Some learnt to share their genetic heritage by becoming multi-celled sexual creatures. This was another huge evolutionary leap, as they bequeathed to their progeny an extravagance of possibilities. Creativity expanded rapidly throughout Earth's waters; worms and jellyfish appeared.

### The Human Body
From conception through to embryo to fully-formed fetus to mature adult, our bodies are extraordinary achievements of Nature. The body has 78 organs – including the brain, heart, hands, stomach and reproductive organs. We are made up of 11 essential chemicals –including oxygen, carbon, hydrogen, calcium, phosphorus. We are 60% water, and have 200 bones, framed to hold us together and protect our organs. The body is somewhat like a well-run city, with the brain as the city manager operating a highly efficient information network through the nervous

system. The brain has 86 billion nerve cells (neurons) – our 'grey matter'. These connect to billions of nerve fibres by trillions of connections (synapses). The body itself has 30 trillion cells, each with its own structure and function. The *endocrine* system (*endo* = within, *krino* = sifting) is made up of *glands* that make hormones (*hormone* = to stir up). They are the body's chemical messengers.

Our energy comes through our respiratory and digestive systems. Lungs take in air and extract from it life-giving oxygen, using descendants of the first symbiotic cells described earlier. They expel carbon dioxide. The mouth takes in food and drink and with the help of a 30-foot digestive tract, converts it into energy. The cardio-vascular system circulates the blood and provides nutrients. The immune system is always on standby when the body is in distress.

While eventually the whole body system breaks down and we become a handful of dust, we believe that God transforms us and raises us to new and everlasting life. How this will be we do not know. But the gospel writers have left us with two resurrection images to play with: we are to be *born again* and we are to be *raised up in glory*, a glory in which all Creation will share.

*'The Lord God formed humans from the dust of the ground and breathed into their nostrils the breath of life, and they became living beings'.*

(Gen 2:7)

# 'WOW! WHAT HAPPENED NEXT?'

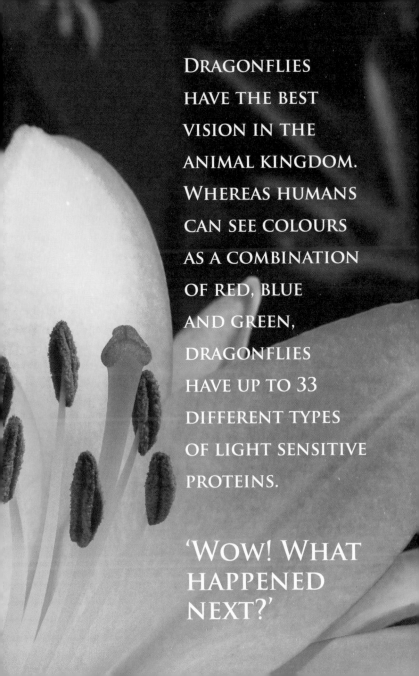

DRAGONFLIES
HAVE THE BEST
VISION IN THE
ANIMAL KINGDOM.
WHEREAS HUMANS
CAN SEE COLOURS
AS A COMBINATION
OF RED, BLUE
AND GREEN,
DRAGONFLIES
HAVE UP TO 33
DIFFERENT TYPES
OF LIGHT SENSITIVE
PROTEINS.

'WOW! WHAT
HAPPENED
NEXT?'

# STEP 11
# FISH AND SIGHT

## 525,000,000 years ago

Fish evolved from sea-squirts, and backbones encased the earliest nervous systems.

Fish gradually took over from invertebrates (creatures without backbones). The latter lived in the sea whereas the vertebrates adapted their fins into rudimentary legs, so that eventually they could crawl to land as reptiles and raise their bodies to move about (*reptilis* = creeping).

Deep in the oceans the light-sensitive eyespots in some fish species evolved into eyes. Earth, blind until then, saw herself for the first time through the eyes of fish! But today two-thirds of the world's fish species are currently over-exploited and endangered.

*Eyesight*
By studying the light-sensitive structures in existing species, scientists constructed hypotheses about how complex eyes like ours developed. They may have first evolved from the simple light-sensitive spots on the skins of some

creatures, whereby outside information was taken in. Successive changes may have created a depression in the light-sensitive patch, a deepening pit that made 'vision' a little sharper, rather like a pinhole camera. Eventually, the light-sensitive spot became a retina – the layer of cells and pigment at the back of the human eye – and over time a lens formed at the front.

It took millions of years for the human eye as we know it to emerge. Some other creatures developed sharper sight than ourselves. Certain owls can pinpoint a mouse a kilometer away even when only candle-light is available. Pythons and boas have our eyesight but also can see infrared light: in the dark they can pinpoint prey from their body heat. Bees see ultraviolet light and can navigate from the position of the sun even when it is cloudy.

Other insects see a riot of colour beyond anything we can imagine. Of these, dragonflies have the best vision in the animal kingdom. Whereas humans can see colours as a combination of red, blue and green, dragonflies have up to 33 different types of light sensitive proteins. This keen eyesight enables them to be the most successful predator on the planet. Their bulbous eyes are made up of up to 30,000 facets, each pointing in a slightly different direction, enabling them to see in many directions at the same time.

*'When the Lord is revealed, we shall be like him, because we shall see him as he is'.* (1 Jn 3:2)

# 'WOW! WHAT HAPPENED NEXT?'

# STEP 12
# PLANTS AND ANIMALS

## 460,000,000 years ago

Leaving the security of their swamps, worms, mollusks, and crustaceans took to our shores, developed the capacity to breathe on land, to survive weather extremes, to resist gravity and to defend themselves. Algae and fungi ventured ashore as well, and the first plants evolved as mosses.

### Land and Rock

What is the ground beneath our feet made of? Land is a thin layer of clay or soil with rocks underneath. Below that is bedrock, hard, thick and solid. Ireland has a great variety of bedrock, dating from 1.8 billion to about 300 million years ago. The upper part of our island belonged originally to an earlier continent, which eventually became North America: the lower part belonged to another continent from which Europe emerged. A great ocean separated the two continents until these collided 420 million years ago, and the land that became Ireland was pushed up close to the equator. A sea extended across Ireland, enabling the formation of sedimentary rocks such as sandstone and mudstone. From 350 to 300 million years ago the shallow warm waters acted as home to shellfish. As these died the shells sank down, creating vast limestone deposits which were changed into rock. Fossils of shellfish are frequently found in limestone.

Rocks are God's old notebooks! *Laudato Si'* adds, 'Soil, water, mountains: everything is, as it were, a caress of God' (LS, 84). Whether on the shore or in cliffs or in the form of gravel, each stone carries a lengthy history. We can admire its silent mystery. The timeline for understanding the humblest rock in a bog is immense. Carlos Drummond's deceptively simple poem, abbreviated here, points to the mystery encased even in a random stone: 'In the middle of the road there was a stone / there was a stone in the middle of the road … Never should I forget this event … Never should I forget that in the middle of the road / there was a stone.'

Earlier you were invited to chat with a leaf; now pick up a stone and imagine what it might wish to say? What can it teach you about the mystery of existence?

*'Lord, what variety you have created, arranging everything so wisely! Earth is full of the things you have made; among them the vast expanse of the oceans, teeming with countless creatures, great and small'.* (Ps 114:24–25)

# 'WOW! WHAT HAPPENED NEXT?'

# Step 13
# Five Mass Extinctions of Species

## From 444,000,000 years ago

Fossil experts identify mass extinctions when large proportions of known species suddenly go missing from the global fossil record. Most extinctions were connected to rapid climate change.

*444,000,000 years ago, 86% of species lost*: A short, severe ice age lowered sea levels, possibly triggered by the uplift of the Appalachians, of which the newly exposed silicate rock sucked $CO_2$ out of the atmosphere, chilling the planet.

*375,000,000 years ago, 75% of species lost:* An example of a lost species is the Trilobite, the most diverse and abundant of the animals that had appeared 550 million years ago. These survived the first great extinction but were nearly wiped out in the second, possibly because newly evolved land plants stirred up the earth, releasing nutrients into the ocean which triggered algal blooms which in turn sucked oxygen out of the water, suffocating bottom dwellers like the Trilobites.

*251,000,000 years ago, 96% of species lost:* This third and worst extinction removed 300,000,000 years' worth of evolutionary diversification. It was caused by a cataclysmic eruption near Siberia that blasted out $CO_2$: global temperatures surged and oceans acidified, emitting poisonous hydrogen sulphide.

*200,000,000 years ago, 80% of species lost*: No clear cause has been found for this extinction.

*66,000,000 years ago, 76% of all species lost:* The Ammonite is an example. Its shell provided it with the fortification required to withstand the pressure of deep dives in pursuit of its prey. While dinosaurs ruled the land during this time, the oceans belonged to the ammonites. They mostly perished together.

Between five and ten million years are needed for Nature to renew Earth with new species. This means that 200,000 generations of humankind must pass before we recover the biodiversity we are currently destroying.

*'Animals, creeping things and birds of the air were blotted out from the earth. But God remembered Noah and the creatures whom he had shut into the ark'.*
(Gen 7 and 8)

# 'WOW! WHAT HAPPENED NEXT?'

# STEP 14
# FLYING INSECTS

## 400,000,000 years ago

Insects evolved with nearly weightless bodies that permitted them to take to the air as the first flying creatures.

### The Butterfly

Let's look at the monarch butterfly, the lord of the insect world. It develops from a tiny egg, becomes a caterpillar, forms a chrysalis (*chrysalis* = golden coloured) and finally transforms into a beautiful butterfly. The milkweed juices it assimilates make it poisonous to birds, and its beautiful orange color warns predators of its toxicity.

The female monarch lays about 400 eggs on milkweed plants. These take two weeks to develop, after which the caterpillar's head becomes visible. The insect is now only 2mm long, but eats voraciously, first its own eggshell, then the milkweed. It eats day and night, stopping only to rest between meals. On its first day it consumes its own weight in food.

Next it leaves the milkweed plant and looks for a safe

place to undergo a profound transformation. Using a special gland in its mouth to weave a small silk button underneath a twig or leaf, it hangs upside down in the shape of a 'J'. In time it begins to move, forcing the skin to split open. It then looks like a giant green water droplet, and slowly changes shape and color. The outer layer hardens into an elegant emerald case, decorated with golden dots. This case is known as a chrysalis. Inside, three different hormones break down the pupa almost completely, only to recreate and enable it to have a different diet, habitat and movement than before.

When the wings are dry the monarch takes to the air. Energy for flying comes from the flowers it visits. Each autumn, huge clouds of monarch butterflies gather in southern Canada and fly south some 3000km to Mexico. Each insect makes the journey only once but manages to pass on the needed navigational information for the grandchild to get to where its grandmother has been.

Insects are essential to many forms of life, but due to pesticides and population growth numbers are now plummeting. We must preserve pollinators!

*'God created every winged bird of every kind'.*
(Gen 1:21)

# 'WOW! WHAT HAPPENED NEXT?'

# STEP 15
# FORESTS

## 335,000,000 years ago

Forests breathe for us because they absorb carbon dioxide $(CO_2)$ and so are vital to our survival. The vast early forests loaded themselves with carbon and became fossilised as coal and oil. Bogs also grow from decayed vegetation and are reservoirs of $CO_2$. This is why coal, oil and turf should be left in peace.

*Trees*
Trees have been described as God's first temples. Like monks they stay put, don't talk much but get on with inner growth. While they work hard for us and for the environment, they also form a 'wood-wide web' of mutual communication and support through fungal interconnections. Mother trees talk with their kin, injured ones pass on their legacy to their neighbours; the healthy support the weak and give out warning signals when under threat. So when a giraffe starts nibbling an acacia tree, the tree gives off an unpleasant gas: acacias close by pick up the

message and pump unpalatable toxins into their leaves, so the hungry giraffe has to lunch elsewhere.

A lesson here is that trees can smell! And when a caterpillar nibbles a leaf, electrical signals are emitted by the tree to ward off further damage. If the root is under attack, helpful fungi spread the word: their thin filaments are densely woven through the soil – one teaspoon of soil contains many miles of 'underground internet cable'. In this way, nutrients can be shared out to best advantage. An Oregon fungus is 2400 years old, extends 3000 acres and weighs 660 tons.

Trees grow at a leisurely pace: they know all about ripening in old age! Redwoods may live 2000 years. But imagine the amount of energy, know-how and organisation a large tree needs: food and water supplies must be secure, wood beetles must be warded off, offspring must be attended to. A big tree is a community housing project: some 250 species may lodge in it – bats, woodpeckers, parasites. These may do damage to their host-trees but currently their worst enemy is the human species. Tree planting is essential if we are to survive.

*'God said, "Are the trees in the fields*
*human beings, that they should*
*come under siege from you?"'*
(Deut 20:19)

# 'WOW! WHAT HAPPENED NEXT?'

# STEP 16
# DINOSAURS AND OTHER REPTILES

## 235,000,000 years ago

Dinosaurs (*dinosaur* = fearfully great reptile) first appeared 245 million years ago, in the Jurassic Age. They explored the extremes of size, speed and strength and ruled the Earth for 175 million years until they were wiped out 66 million years ago in the Fifth Mass Extinction. Only those dinosaur species that gave rise to birds survived. The extinction was due to a triple disastrous event, involving asteroid impact, choking chemicals from volcanoes and climate change due to the lengthy blocking out of the sun.

Some dinosaurs attained 20 metres (65 feet) in height, equal to a seven-storey building. Giraffes, in contrast, are only 20 feet tall. Dinosaurs weighed up to 77 tonnes – equivalent to 14 elephants. Their length was 40 metres or 120 feet. Only whales have ever matched their bulk. Their biggest eggs were about 12 inches long, weighed about 15 pounds and held a half-gallon of contents. Some dinosaurs were hunters: as bipeds they could use their forelegs to forage and exploit a world of forests.

One branch, the Sauropods, were herbivores with long heads, necks and tails. They were among the largest land animals ever, but it appears that they had small brains. Some were gentle leaf-eating giants. The big, classic dinosaurs are extinct, but birds are living descendants of dinosaurs. Imagine a chicken fluffed-up to dinosaur dimensions! Fossils show that some dinosaurs had feathers or feather-like body covering, but many of them didn't fly and probably didn't even glide. Instead, feathers likely helped these bird-like dinosaurs stay warm as juveniles or send signals to other individuals.

Only two dinosaur bones have been discovered in Ireland because most of our rocks pre-date the dinosaur era. Also Ireland was underwater for significant portions of time when dinosaurs ruled the planet.

Below the surface of the world's oceans a lot else was happening during this time. Marine fish and reptiles abounded, including tuna and dolphin-shaped ocean-going predators. These largely went extinct about 150 million years ago.

*'The Lord said, "Look at Behemoth – its bones are tubes of iron, its limbs like bars of iron – only its Maker can approach it"'*. (Job 40:19)

# 'WOW! WHAT HAPPENED NEXT?'

# STEP 17
# MAMMALS

## 200,000,000 years ago

Mammals (*mamma* = breast or teat) evolved from ancestral reptiles. Reptiles are cold-blooded and depend on the sun's heat for energy, whereas mammals are warm-blooded, generate their own heat and can move around more freely. The first mammals were small and nocturnal insect-eaters who learned to jump, climb, swing, and swim through a world of giants. The emergence of mammals was a triumph of Nature's capacity for adaptation.

There were other remarkable developments. While reptiles entrust their nests of well-stocked eggs to hatch and develop on their own, birds emerged which laid much smaller eggs, watched over them and cared for the chicks when hatched. Again, some mammals began to produce eggs within their bodies and provided them with a nurturing environment until they were ready to be born. They then invested enormous energy in caring for their offspring. Think of today's cows, cats and sows. They fed them with their own milk, which is rich in protein, carbohydrates and fats. This strategy called lactation (*lac* = milk), enabled mothers in the wild to spend more time in the burrow or nest, where they kept their young fed and warm, instead of having to go hunting. Gradually mammals took over the world and we humans derive from them.

Mammals are also characterised by the evolution of relatively large brains. It has been proposed that there is a threefold evolution of the human brain, from reptilian to mammalian to human – the neo-cortex. We need the three layers, but if mammalian and nurturing care is poor or almost absent, an individual is deprived of the capacity for bonding, relationship and love. When the reptilian instinct for survival links with the reasoning capacity, but without the intervening level of affectivity, a toxic combination results, and may explain appalling behavior for which the individual may not be fully morally responsible.

*'Can a woman forget her nursing child, or show no compassion for the child of her womb?'*
(Isa 49:15)

# 'WOW! WHAT HAPPENED NEXT?'

# STEP 18
# BIRDS AND FLOWERS

## 150,000,000 years ago

Birds evolved from a sub-group of ancestral dinosaurs, and Earth broke into song. Earth also adorned herself in colorful and fragrant flowers irresistible to insects. Birds and flowers are among the creatures that draw our universal respect. Imagine a silent and colorless world such as was portrayed by Rachel Carson in her *Silent Spring*! But a quarter of the world's bird species have been wiped out in recent years, so bird conservation is a pressing concern.

The variety of flowering plants is enormous and glorious. *Laudato Si'* notes that that all creatures have their own purpose, they are not simply for us, and their multiplicity and variety expresses something of the nature of God (LS, 83; 86).

In spring and summer flowers emerge and fruit trees burst into blossom. They gladden our hearts but also use their beauty of colour and form to attract pollinators, else they would not produce the seeds needed to survive as a species. Different colours and shapes attract different pollinators – bees, butterflies etc. When pollination is complete, flowers drop their advertising strategies and fade, but while doing so they produce seeds. When these mature they need to be dispersed, either by wind or water, or by hitching a ride from some passing creature. Think of the lowly dandelion as its yellow face transforms into a downy head of seeds, each with a little parachute to sail off to a destination unknown. The fruit which may encase the seed – as in apples and haws – attracts birds and animals: they eat the fruit and deposit the inedible seeds at random. Delicate orchid seeds need a particular fungal association to give them lodging till they mature.

Each species has evolved its own distinctive methods of family planning, else it would have disappeared long ago. The most attractive flowers attract the most insects, so we must defend our insect pollinators in order that flowers may continue to radiate their beauty.

*Jesus said: "Consider the ravens; they neither sow nor reap, they have neither storehouse nor barn, and yet God feeds them. And consider the lilies, how they grow: they neither spin nor weave, yet I tell you that even Solomon in all his glory was not clothed like one of these"'.*
(Lk 12:24–27)

# 'WOW! WHAT HAPPENED NEXT?'

# STEP 19
# THE CARNIVAL
# OF THE ANIMALS

## 60,000,000 years ago

After the Fifth Mass Extinction, 66 million years ago, when the dominating dinosaurs had disappeared, Nature got to work again.

Surviving small mammals began to evolve rapidly and diversify into a wide range of habitats. Earth greeted rodents, monkeys, horses, cats and dogs, elephants, chimpanzees, camels, bears and pigs.

*Water*
Fresh water was vital for the survival and development of all these species. A horse needs 5–10 gallons a day, while an elephant needs a full bathtub – 50 gallons. So what is water?

The chemical formula $H_2O$ means that one *molecule* of *water* is composed of two hydrogen atoms and one oxygen atom. Simple! But the origins of Earth's water are not yet fully known. A 2018 study suggested that most of our water came from wandering waterlogged asteroids, and that other water molecules, hydrogen and oxygen, came from the solar cloud of gas left over from the formation of the sun. These soggy asteroids had begun developing into planets while the solar nebula still swirled around the sun, so they had water on board. When baby asteroids collided, the bigger ones grew rapidly and eventually a collision introduced enough energy to melt the surface of the largest embryo into an ocean of magma – hot molten rock. This largest embryo eventually became Earth and husbanded a great deal of water. This recent study, if verified, has implications both for the origins of life on Earth and the possibility of life elsewhere in the universe.

All life depends on water. Indeed the wars of the future may be water wars, because the volume of water on Earth and beneath its surface is limited. Our National Holy Wells Day in mid-June is an effort to raise consciousness about water both locally and globally. Following the UN Declaration on Human Rights in 1948 Pope Francis in *Laudato Si'* says that access to safe drinkable water is a basic and universal human right, since it is essential to human survival, and that we have a grave social debt towards the poor who lack access to drinking water (LS, 30).

*'The rain and the snow come down*
*from heaven and do not return there until*
*they have watered the earth'.* (Isa 55: 10)

# 'WOW! WHAT HAPPENED NEXT?'

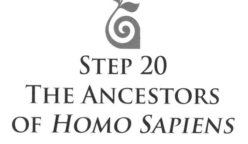

# STEP 20
# THE ANCESTORS
# OF *HOMO SAPIENS*

## 6,000,000 years ago

The Creation Walk is a story of ongoing change, development and novelty. New fossil discoveries and the use of DNA continue to rewrite the complex history of our family tree. Six million years ago saw the last grandparents of humans and chimpanzees. Creatures with ape-like protruding faces, powerful jaws and small brains began to leave the forest, stand up and walk on two legs. The savanna offered challenges and opportunities for these *hominins* – our earliest ancestors – to evolve.

Over millions of years our forebears developed large brains, strong wrists and thumbs, flexible waists, long legs and short toes. Such features supported two defining trends in our evolution: upright movement and the capacity to use tools. Different species emerged. *Homo sapiens* (*Homo* = human, *sapiens* = thinking) evolved in Africa about 200,000 years ago, and had many cousins, but all have vanished. Did our species simply outstrip their cousins or eliminate them as rivals? We do not know.

But we do know some of the tortuous paths by which the development of our species occurred. The discovery of fire 300,000 years ago fostered the social trait of cooperation. Tools date back 200,000 years, a critical milestone in determining the emergence of *Homo sapiens*. Language brought an ever-increasing capacity to share knowledge, to imagine, to experiment and to follow through on results. Watching young children we see that innate curiosity distinguishes human offspring, whereas for other animals consciousness is a part-time employee. Monogamy may also have favoured development, likewise an ideal of justice and fairness, as found in the myriad expressions of the Golden Rule – 'Do to others as you wish them to do to you'.

*Homo sapiens* began to spread from Africa to Australia and to America. This occurred multiple times, most recently about 60,000 years ago. The Neanderthals had been dominant in Europe but went extinct 30,000 years ago. By 13,000 years ago the Cro-Magnon race of *Homo sapiens* was the only surviving human species and began to dominate the world.

*'God created humankind in the divine image: male and female God created them and said to them, be fruitful and multiply and fill the earth'.* (Gen 1:27–28)

# 'WOW! WHAT HAPPENED NEXT?'

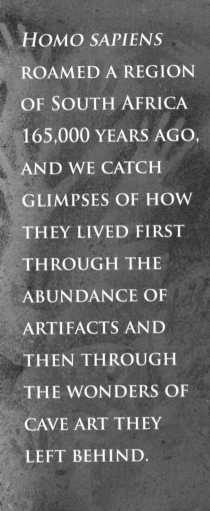

*HOMO SAPIENS* ROAMED A REGION OF SOUTH AFRICA 165,000 YEARS AGO, AND WE CATCH GLIMPSES OF HOW THEY LIVED FIRST THROUGH THE ABUNDANCE OF ARTIFACTS AND THEN THROUGH THE WONDERS OF CAVE ART THEY LEFT BEHIND.

'WOW! WHAT HAPPENED NEXT?'

# STEP 21
# *HOMO SAPIENS*

## 200,000 years ago

*Expansions of Consciousness*

Skeletons of our species date from at least 200,000 years ago. *Homo sapiens* roamed a region of South Africa 165,000 years ago, and we catch glimpses of how they lived first through the abundance of artifacts and then through the wonders of cave art they left behind. The earliest evidence of symbolic expression – creating a shape that stands for something else – dates back 100,000 years. Today we are awash with symbols – highway signs, iPhone icons, wedding rings, tattoos, national flags, but as far back as 36,000 years ago some of our ancestors stood by flickering firelight and began to draw on the bare walls of their caves profiles of cave lions and bears, herds of rhinos and mammoths, horses and ibex, an immense bison – 442 animals in all, done in ochre over a huge period of time and using 400,000 square feet of cave surfaces as canvas. Stenciled handprints are found which send a message: 'I am alive! I was here! I am human. I belong'.

Most of our knowledge of early human development comes from fossil records and tools, so the birth of spoken language remains one of the great mysteries. But with its evolution our species developed the exponentially growing world of knowledge and began to share information, beliefs, experiences and skills. Huge shifts in consciousness and relationships were required to bring this about.

Today through the new cosmology we have more than enough data to bring us to another expansion of consciousness: a sense of the world community of all living things. There emerges hope that we can move beyond wars, rivalries, boundaries and possessiveness. The universe is not ours to control and possess: like the early dwellers on Earth we must emerge from the caves and forests of our tribal mentalities to share with others the vast world around us. The new cosmology provides common ground for us to live in harmony with one another and with all other species.

*'When I look at the heavens, the moon and the stars you have established, what are human beings that you are mindful of them, mortals that you care for them?'*

(Ps 8:3–4)

# 'WOW! WHAT HAPPENED NEXT?'

# STEP 22
# IRELAND'S ICE CAP MELTS

## 16,000 years ago

The last European Ice Age began 1.8 million years ago due to a fall in global temperatures. The resultant ice-cap was some 1000 meters deep and weighed several hundred tonnes per square metre. Our most recent glacier began 30,000 years ago and shaped our landscape with graceful hills, corrie lakes and eskers, and with moraines and drumlins – mounds of gravel left behind by the glacier. The Irish Sea was originally a large freshwater lake: warmer weather brought about rising sea levels so that it became a salt water sea. The Ice Cap also spread that covering of soil that makes Ireland fertile and green: soil or clay is a combination of decayed organic matter from forests and rock materials ground down by the ice.

### The First Irish
The first humans arrived in Ireland 9,000 years ago when the ice-cap was long gone. Their lasting memorials are their burial sites, Newgrange dates back 5,200 years, 700

years before the Egyptian pyramids, and might have taken 300 workers 20 years to construct. Since the dawn of human history humans have honored their dead with mourning, proper burial, care of tombs and have nourished hope, however dimly perceived, of an afterlife.

The Hebrews believed that the dead were gathered as shadows in Sheol, without life or hope. While they yearned that God's faithfulness might restore the just to life forever, hope for immortality awaited proof. Seen in this context, Jesus' promise to his hearers that eternal life could be theirs was astounding. Even more astounding was his own resurrection from the dead, which was understood as being not for himself alone but for all. Billions of our ancestors have died, and so shall we, but in Christian belief death is now only the passageway to everlasting life. Perhaps the passage grave and burial chamber at Newgrange, which is illuminated by dawn sunlight for 17 minutes annually, already hinted at this hope.

*Job said: "I know that my Redeemer lives, and I will see God for myself, and not as a stranger. How my heart yearns within me!"*
(Job 19:25–27)

# 'WOW! WHAT HAPPENED NEXT?'

# STEP 23
# AGRICULTURE

## 11,000 years ago

Early humans were hunter-gatherers: they gathered wild fruits and hunted animals. Slowly the more manageable species were domesticated: goats, horses, camels; wheat, rice, peas, lentils, olives and grapes. Our cuisine today is basically that of our ancient farming predecessors.

### Stewardship of the Earth

*Laudato Si'* reminds us that since everything has a value of its own in God's eyes, we are called to be stewards, custodians, trustees or guardians of Nature but never its dominators. We are to reflect the divine care that cherishes all Creation (LS, 67–69), and to till and keep – that is, cultivate and protect – the gift loaned to us by God (Gen 2:15). Ecology is thus firmly located in the realm of the sacred, and God's preferential care for the poor and marginalised of this world is now seen to embrace the oppressed species which we carelessly destroy.

Reading the parable of the Good Samaritan today,

therefore, we must include both our injured and despoiled neighbor and all of Creation. The wounded and half-dead traveler in the story can stand for Mother Earth, and we are to be the Samaritans that bind her wounds, pouring in oil and wine, carrying her to safety and bearing the cost of her recovery (Lk 10:25–37).

As humans we need to learn the self-sacrificing rhythms of Nature, where receiving and giving is the central dynamic. Growth and decay, living and dying, are an interwoven cycle. The air molecules that fill our lungs were breathed by others before us – by animals and humans, by women and men, by saints and sinners, by the small and great, by Jesus and Mohammed! Nature is the ultimate genius for recycling, and everything is in process of becoming something else.

This is the dance of Creation. The philosopher Nietzsche (1844–1900) who coined the phrase 'the death of God' remarked, 'I would believe only in a god that knows how to dance'. The theologian Leonardo Boff confidently states that at the close of history we will sing and dance forever with God and the created world.

*'The Lord God put human beings in the garden of Eden to till it and keep it. Abel was a keeper of sheep, and Cain a tiller of the ground'.*
(Gen 2:15; 4:2)

# 'WOW! WHAT HAPPENED NEXT?'

# STEP 24
# EMPIRES AND RELIGIONS

## 5,000 years ago

Agriculture led to collaboration and to cities. In the Near East empires emerged and disappeared: the Sumerian, Egyptian, Assyrian, Babylonian, Greek, Persian, Roman.

The Major Religions began to emerge—Hinduism (c. 2000 BC), Judaism (1250 BC), Confucianism (550 BC), Buddhism (500 BC), Christianity, (first century AD). Islam came later (AD 60).

### The Hebrew Story

The Hebrew story originates with a Hebrew slave in Egypt about 1250 BC. Moses, a criminal turned shepherd, experienced himself being spoken to out of a burning bush. The mysterious speaker knew the name that had been given him by Pharaoh's daughter. When Moses asked, *'Who are you?'* the reply was both profound and puzzling: *'I am who I am. I just am'*. Fascinated, he was told to come no closer, but to take off his sandals, because the patch of desert he was standing on was *'holy ground'*. Moses, a nonentity with a dark past, was then commissioned to liberate his people in the name and power of this Being, to whom the Hebrews gave the name Yahweh (see, Ex 3).

In epic stories the Hebrews attributed their liberation and subsequent history to *'the One who simply is'*. Later they judged that Creation itself must also be the work of Yahweh, and so they devised the Genesis stories, written between the tenth and sixth century BC. Through political upheavals and religious oppressions, the tiny land of Israel survived and clung to its faith in Yahweh.

The primary focus of the Hebrew Bible, however, is less on Creation than on God's activity in the world. Yahweh has a single great plan of salvation, embracing human and cosmic history from creation to consummation. As Creator, Liberator and Redeemer, the One who simply is will shepherd home not only the Hebrews but all peoples.

*'From one ancestor God made all nations to inhabit the earth, so that they would search for and find God, though indeed God is not far from any of us'.*
(Acts 17:26–27)

# 'WOW! WHAT HAPPENED NEXT?'

# STEP 25
# THE NEW CREATION

## 2,000 years ago

In the Christian view Jesus is not simply a religious leader among others, but the One who brings the process of evolution to an entirely new level.

'The Christian view is that the Next Step (in evolution) has already appeared. And it is really new. It is not a change from brainy into brainier people: it is a change that goes off in a totally different direction – a change from being creatures to being sons and daughters of God. The first instance appeared in Palestine two thousand years ago' – C S Lewis.

Jesus emerges from the shadows of pre-history as the One who is both human and divine. He is presented as 'the light of the world' and invites all humankind to share his divinity. He proclaims a kingdom based on mutual forgiveness, inclusion and love. With his resurrection from death begins the divinising of humankind and of all Creation (LS, 236; Romans 8:21).

*The New Testament*

Compiled soon after the time of Jesus, the Christian Bible or New Testament is an effort to convey God's extraordinary intentions for humankind. St Paul states it simply: '*When anyone is in Christ, there is a new creation*' (2 Cor 5:17). This '*new creation*' is spelled out as eternal divine companionship.

The New Testament is the best-selling book of all time and the most fought-over. It offers profound and hope-filled enlightenment on the ultimate meaning of human existence. God's creative and redeeming activity as revealed in Jesus overarches all else: '*I have come that people may have life, life to the full*' (Jn 10:10). '*Life to the full*' means everlasting life. This central message of hope is carried in short phrases scattered like jewels across its pages. We discover that we were chosen out before the Creation Walk ever began, and invited to live through love in the divine presence. More than a set of beliefs, Christian faith is interpersonal and brings us into a network of divine relationships. The divine is already disguised in the human and in due time will burst forth in glory.

*'To all who received him Jesus gave power to become children of God. We will be like God because we will see him as he is'.*
(Jn 1:12; 1 Jn 3:2)

# 'WOW! WHAT HAPPENED NEXT?'

# Step 26
# Irish Christianity

## 1600 years ago

### Island of Saints and Scholars

We know that Christianity had come to Ireland before St Patrick because Palladius was sent about AD 430 'to the Irish (already) believing in Christ'. Patrick came as bishop in 432, and worked for 30 years, leaving behind a thriving Christian community, which supplanted the ancient druidic religion. Monasticism began to flourish; some 1600 monastic remains are extant, and over 3000 Holy Wells. In the seventh century reforming monks began to live as hermits: an austere community lived on the Skellig Islands until the thirteenth century. The monks found God in the beauty of their surroundings, and Europe's earliest nature poetry emerged.

Monastic scholarship attracted students from abroad, while Irish monks played a large role in the evangelisation of Europe, and preserved the remains of classical civilisation during the Dark Ages (AD 500–1000). From the ninth century onward Vikings pillaged Irish monasteries, and in the twelfth century St Malachy of Armagh labored to reform the weakened Church.

*Faith of our Predecessors*
In 1154 Henry II of England was authorised by the English-born Pope Adrian IV to invade Ireland 'to proclaim the truths of the Christian religion to a rude and ignorant people'. In 1542 Henry VIII ordered the closure of all monasteries. The (Protestant) Church of Ireland was established. Penal Laws, 1691–1829, were designed to force Irish Catholics to convert to Protestantism and to abandon the Irish language. Catholics were dispossessed, the clergy had a price on their heads and Mass rocks replaced churches. In the eighteenth and nineteenth century religious congregations were established by Nano Nagle, Ignatius Rice, Catherine McAuley, Mary Aikenhead and Margaret Aylward. After Catholic Emancipation in 1829 Cardinal Cullen brought the Irish Church under Roman discipline. The Apparition at Knock took place in 1879. The challenge to Christians today is to radiate divine love to humankind and to Creation. A more loving and compassionate world community is to be our goal.

*'In the wilderness the Lord your God carried you, just as one carries a child, all the way that you travelled until you reached this place. The Lord goes before you to show you the route you should take'.* (Deut 1:31–33).

# 'WOW! WHAT WILL HAPPEN NEXT?'

# STEP 27
# THE ANTHROPOCENE ERA

## 250 years ago

The Anthropocene Era (*anthropos* = human, *cene* = recent) is the term given by some scholars to the present era which began with the Industrial Revolution, about 1750. Manufacturing of goods moved from small shops and homes to large factories, to machinery and mass production. People had to move to cities for work and so became alienated from their birthplaces and skills, from the items they produced and also from Nature. They became anonymous cogs serving the great machine of progress. Engines, coal, oil, iron and steel dominated, and transport became the key to new markets.

We humans began to re-engineer the planet for our own purposes, and do so still. The quality of life has improved for many, but at huge cost to Nature, to the poor and to human relationships.

The documentary film *Anthropocene* examines how humans recklessly drain life from the planet as they pillage its resources. In Kenya tens of thousands of elephant tusks are shown discarded as mementoes of human greed and wastefulness. In Germany the world's largest excavation rig reduces entire villages into coal mines. The battering ram of industry and corporate power turns lives and histories into rubble. *Anthropocene* implores us to look at the world anew and to realize that Earth's beauty isn't ours for the taking. The London Zoo features sullen endangered animals, who don't deserve the fate to which we condemn them.

Consumerism, unbridled capitalism, the profit motive and the myth of unlimited progress are behind our current crisis. Y N Yahari in *Homo Deus* (*homo* = human, *deus* = God) notes how Silicon Valley bewitches us with promises of happiness, peace, prosperity and even life after death. We have indeed vast creativity and know-how, but because we lack the vision of what humankind is meant to be, we don't manage them well.

*'The rich man said, "I will pull down my barns and build larger ones,, and I will say to my soul, Soul, you have ample goods laid up for many years; relax, eat, drink, be merry", but God said to him, "this very night your life is being demanded of you. And the things you have prepared, whose will they be?"'*. (Lk 12:18–20)

## 'WOW! WHAT WILL HAPPEN NEXT?'

# STEP 28
# OUR EXPANDING UNIVERSE

## 90 years ago

In the early 1930s Edwin Hubble (1889–1953) provided evidence that the galaxies were moving apart at an increasing speed. Earth was revealed as a microscopic speck in an unimportant corner of an ever-expanding universe.

Astro-physicists were able to work back to the starting point of this phenomenon. Their consensus is that in an infinitesimal moment of time after the Big Bang the universe suddenly expanded and increased in volume by a factor of at least $10^{78}$, equivalent to expanding an object which is about half the width of a molecule of DNA in length to one approximately 10.6 light years long, or 62 trillion miles. A much slower and gradual expansion continued after this, until at around 9.8 billion years after the Big Bang the universe began to expand more quickly. It is still doing so, like dough rising in a hot oven.

From 1946 onward, partial images of Earth were seen from space. The first time we saw the *whole* Earth from outside was with Apollo 8 in 1968. A new global consciousness is emerging of the fragile beauty of Planet Earth, and of the challenge to foster a world community of compassion and mutual care.

In the 1960's Cosmic Microwave Background Radiation was discovered. It appears that when the universe was very young – only 500,000 years old – stars and galaxies had not yet formed: the universe consisted of a hot soup of electrons and atomic nuclei, with a background thermal radiation of over 3000 °C. Soon after this time the universe expanded and the background radiation cooled enough for the electrons to combine with the nuclei to form atoms which grew into the galaxies and clusters we now see. That radiation from 13.3 billion year ago can still be detected today. It is estimated that as yet we understand only some 4% of the reality in which we are immersed: dark matter is the next puzzle for our astrophysicists to solve!

*'The Lord says, "I know the plans I have in mind for you; plans for peace, not disaster, reserving a future full of hope for you"'.*
(Jer 29:11)

# 'WOW! WHAT WILL HAPPEN NEXT?'

# STEP 29
# A SMALL BLUE PLANET

## 50 years ago

Many astronauts report a cognitive shift when they view Earth from above. In October 2017 the crew of the International Space Station chatted with Pope Francis: one said that what he most enjoyed was being able to see God's Creation maybe a little bit from God's perspective. He added that you could not but be touched in your soul at the indescribable beauty of the Earth, turning peacefully on its axis without borders or conflict; so awesomely beautiful and fragile.

Russell Sweickart in 1969, expressed the reflections which follow.

*The astronaut looks back and sees the Earth not as something big but small. And now the contrast between Earth – that bright blue-and-white Christmas tree ornament – and that black sky, that infinite universe, really comes through. Earth becomes so small and so fragile, and such a precious little spot in the universe, and you realise that on that small spot, that little blue-and-white thing, is everything that means anything to you; all of history, music, poetry, art, games, war and death, birth and love, tears and joy, all of it is on that little spot out there that you can cover with your thumb.*

*You're going 25,000 mph, ripping through a vacuum, and there's not a sound. There's a silence, the depth of which you've never experienced before, and you think about what you're experiencing and why. Have you been separated out by God to have some special experience that other people cannot have? No.*

*It's not for yourself. You have to bring it back, somehow – a rather special responsibility. It tells you something about your relationship with this life. When you come back, there's a difference – so precious – in the relationship between you and that planet and all its forms of life, because you've had that kind of experience.*

**'If I go up to heaven, you are there; if I ride the wings of the morning, if I dwell by the farthest oceans, even there your hand will guide me and your strength will support me'.**
(Ps 139:8–10)

## 'WOW! WHAT WILL HAPPEN NEXT?'

# STEP 30
# THE GOD OF GALAXIES, GLOW-WORMS AND GRACE

## Now and Forever

Creation manifests the divine. The divine can be encountered in sub-atomic particles, in the world of Nature, and in deep space (Rom 1:19–20; LS, 18). As we explore our world we find that the divine is inventive, dynamic, pulsating, unpredictable. A great fountain of love, beauty and energy are endlessly being poured out on vast galaxies and on tiny fairy-flies and on ourselves.

Early Christian theologians struggled to offer an image of the Author of Creation. Rather than picturing the three divine Persons seated on thrones – as were the emperors and their consorts of that time – they chose the image of dance to suggest a glorious procession of mutual love, a whirling and joyous ecstasy. We may imagine heaven, not as an endless choir practice on a wet Sunday afternoon, but as the unrestricted and all-inclusive joy of dancing in a transfigured universe.

We are part of the unfathomable weave of the universe,

immersed in its deep mystery. Its dance has already begun: it has always been in process. Each of us has a role in it. Jesus and his Father are working (Jn 4:34) for the good of all Creation and we can tune in to their signals and do likewise. Thomas Merton says that every moment and every event in every person's life plants seeds of spiritual vitality in their hearts. This is the divine at work on Earth: this is grace, and grace is everywhere. All is sacred, and so are we. We must not desecrate our Common Home. We belong to the great Creation Story, to a whole that is infinitely greater than ourselves. We are called even now to share with all of Creation '*in the freedom of the children of God*' (Rom 8:21).

So let's put on our dancing shoes and learn the steps of the cosmic dance!

*'See, the home of God is among mortals. God will dwell with them and they will be God's people'.*
(Rev 21:3)

# 'WOW! WHAT WILL HAPPEN NEXT?'

# PART THREE

# WHAT HOPE FOR
# A SMALL BLUE PLANET?

# WHAT HOPE FOR A SMALL BLUE PLANET?

We have sketched what is currently known of the environmental and biological history of the cosmos over the past 13.8 billion years. Planet Earth came into being only some 4 billion years ago and has a finite future: scientists say that in some two billion years it will begin to fry. But in the meantime it will become less and less habitable due to climate overheating and human destructiveness. The planet itself may survive, but will there be life upon it? Will only a small number of species, such as the resilient bacteria-like organisms we have considered earlier, survive the Sixth Mass Extinction which is already upon us? Will anyone of the human species be there to see what will remain?

An abundance of scientific data illustrates our current crisis. Wallace-Wells in *The Uninhabitable Earth* lists the following: heat death, hunger, drowning, wildfires, loss of fresh water, plagues and illnesses, dying oceans, unbreathable air, economic collapse, climate conflict.

On the positive side, there is an ever-growing global community of concern, shown in local and international ways; youth demonstrations such as those headed by Greta Thunberg have their own effect. Across cultures and religious beliefs movers and shakers are hard at work. Science offers hope through the development of wind and solar energy, new forms of transport, strategies to reduce pollution. While multiple uncertainties operate within the universe because of the randomness and chaos built into its dynamics, decisions must be based on the best evidence, even at costly commitment.

The rich are hurt least and last by planetary disasters, while the poor are hurt first and worst; but we are all part of the problem and carry responsibility to generate the solution on micro and macro levels. Global compassion for the disenfranchised must grow: you can vote, you can speak, you can put your body on the line, you can pray. Shallow optimism that science or God or both will sort things out will not do: nor will passive fatalism, 'collapsology' is a new term which captures this mood.

We already touched at the end of part one on the meaning of hope in the Christian tradition. We can think of hope as divine energy given to sustain us even in the most unpromising situations. Because hope is from God and focused on God it has an indestructible quality that carries us beyond failure, frustration and dead ends. We badly need such hope. So let us now look more deeply into the vast resources in the Christian tradition that ground hope for our future. Again it must be stressed that Christian hope is not to be used as a crutch but as an inspiration to do all we can in the belief that God is directing our decision making and enabling it to be fruitful. I pick seven lines of exploration: there are many more but space forbids! Scripture references enable you to follow up quotations at greater depth for yourself or in group-work.

# 1: THE GOD OF SMALL THINGS

Our efforts may seem small and futile, but many gospel episodes reveal the recurring motif, that God has an eye for small people and small things. Think of the mustard seed, the widow's mite and the multiplication of the loaves and fish (Mk 4:31; 12:41–44; 8:1–9). At Cana dull water is turned into the best of wine (Jn 2:1–12); at the Last Supper lowly bread and wine become the body and blood of the Lord (Lk 22:19–20). The life of each person, no matter how hidden, has its influence on all others (Rom 14:7). Any good deed, however small, that is done in love has an eternal quality, because love does not come to an end (1 Cor 13:8) and we will reap its reward at harvest time (Gal 6:9). This grounds hope that our tiny contributions on behalf of our sick planet carry their own symbolic value. Julian of Norwich expresses this hope:

*God showed me a little thing, the size of a hazel nut, lying in the palm of my hand. I looked upon it and thought, 'What may this be?' And I was answered, 'It is all that is made.' I marveled how it might last, for I thought it might suddenly have fallen to nothing for smallness. And I was answered, 'It lasts and ever shall, for God loves it. And so have all things their beginning by the love of God'. In this little thing I saw three truths: the first is that God made it; the second that God loves it; and the third that God keeps it safe.*

# 2: *LAUDATO SI'* SPEAKS OF HOPE

*Laudato Si'* has channeled massive energy into care of our Common Home. Pope Francis shares with all humankind the crucified Christ's challenge to St Francis of Assisi in 1205: *'Francis, go and repair my house which as you see is falling into disrepair'.* Note the divine command, *'Go!'* which we touched on in part one! *Laudato Si'* is interwoven with a strong thread of hope, as the following encouraging quotations show:

> *Hope would have us recognise that there is always a way out.*
> (LS, 61)

> *All it takes is one good person to restore hope.*
> (LS, 71)

> *We must speak of the figure of a Father who creates and who alone owns the world.*
> (LS, 74)

> *The God who created the universe out of nothing can also intervene in this world and overcome every form of evil.*
> (LS, 75)

*A spirituality which forgets God as all-powerful and Creator is not acceptable.*
(LS, 75)

*Jesus has taken to himself this material world (LS, 221) ... and through his Incarnation he has incorporated into his person part of the material world, the seed of definitive transformation.*
(LS, 235)

*The ultimate destiny of the universe is in the fullness of God.*
(LS, 83)

*The world is now journeying toward its final perfection.*
*(LS, 80)*

*The Eucharist is itself an act of cosmic love which penetrates all creation, for in the bread of the Eucharist creation is projected towards divinisation, towards its final transfiguration.* (LS, 236)

*We come together to take charge of this home which has been entrusted to us, knowing that all the good which exists here will be taken up into the heavenly feast. Let us sing as we go. May our struggles and our concern for this planet never take away the joy of our hope.*
(LS, 244)

# 3: Divine Power Is at Work

The current global action to protect and restore Planet Earth is being prompted and enabled by the Spirit of God, the Giver of Life: 'The Holy Ghost over the bent / World broods with warm breast and with ah! Bright wings' – Gerard Manley Hopkins SJ. Humankind is not alone, and is not fighting a helpless cause. Prophetic voices from all sides are supporting our unique historical moment of grace and challenge. We are discovering that what seems lost and beyond recovery can come to life again, as with species being rescued from extinction and with the planting of a great green wall of trees across African deserts. The boundless wisdom and dynamics of the universe that have shaped things thus far are available to us: we are not adrift in cosmic isolation but immersed in a sea of divine energy beyond all comprehension. We must do all we can, and pray deeply, and be willing to suffer much, knowing that divine power is at work within us to carry out God's purposes beyond our hopes and dreams (Eph 3:20). In our global crisis we are also witnessing the surprising growth, even if fragile, of the community of humankind. People of all faiths and none are joining hands in the common cause, and this meets God's underlying desire, that we all may be one in universal harmony (Jn 17:11).

The divine plan for Creation remains steady, and with

God all things are possible, including its restoration: (see Acts 3:21). In Genesis, God utters a word and the world is made. With a divine word the world can likewise be re-fashioned. Our God is a saving, creating and restoring God, a God of limitless love who has compassion on all things. Love has always been the key element in God's decisions on the next step for our planet: this love cannot come to an end but will be revealed when God will be '*all in all*' (1 Cor 15:28: Col 3:11).

The divine covenant with Creation endures forever:

*'When the rainbow is seen in the clouds, I will remember my everlasting covenant with every living creature on the earth'.*
(Gen 9:16).

*'When you send forth your Spirit, you renew the face of the earth'.*
(Ps 104:30).

As Bishop Desmond Tutu says, 'Only God knows what's next!'

# 4: GOD MAKES THE BARREN FRUITFUL

The life-giving interventions of God are a central biblical theme. Earth was a formless void until transformed by God's creative act (Gen 1:1). The Flood would have destroyed all life but for the divinely-inspired building of the Ark. The dry bones in Ezekiel's vision are promised life and breath: '*You shall live, and I will place you on your own soil*' (Ez 37:14). Barrenness is transformed into fruitfulness in the wombs of Sarah, Rebecca, Rachel, Hannah and Elizabeth. The Chosen People are at their lowest when Mary of Nazareth conceives her child by divine intervention. In Jesus' ministry the dead are raised, the sick are healed, water is turned into wine, bread and wine become the carriers of divine life. The overarching divine intervention is the raising of Jesus from death to eternal life: this indicates that the dead will rise to everlasting life in the new creation, because God is Lord not of the dead but of the living (Mk 12:27).

The timing of God's interventions is impossible to predict, but they occur when all seems hopeless. Fruitfulness is the divine gift of God that transforms the most impossible of human catastrophes. We have seen that none of the steps in the Creation Walk were predictable: hence the refrain '*Wow! What happened next?*' We are justified in the hope that the final step of the Great Journey will be no less creative, surprising and fruitful.

# 5: THE NEW CREATION HAS BEGUN

The biblical concept of promise underpins the turbulent history of God's people. Abraham, Moses, David and all the great figures of the Hebrew Bible are the carriers of divine promises. Promises are the language of faithful love: they express God's fidelity to humankind throughout time and history. The core of the divine promises is salvation: humans are told what God is going to do, and in divine time the promise is fulfilled. The Bible closes with the promise of nothing less than a new heaven and a new earth! '*The one on the throne said, "See, I am making all things new"*' (Rev 21:1, 5). Note the *present* tense in the last sentence: we are being told that our sorely wounded world is *already* being transformed; newness is not awaiting the end of history.

The first Easter already proclaims the dawn of this new creation. It moves forward every time a person takes Christ seriously: '*So if anyone is in Christ, there is a new creation: everything old has passed away; see, everything has become new*' (2 Cor 5.17; Gal 6:17). Note here the stress on '*everything*'. St Paul can use it because of our human solidarity with Jesus: he is the first fruits and the rest of humankind is incorporated into him, in a bond so tight it can never be broken, as the liturgy puts it (see 1 Cor 15:20–23).

When we are caught by wonder and gratitude for all of this, we find new energy to face the daily struggle for our small blue planet. For the Christian the resurrection of Jesus is the ultimate motivator for our hope. N T Wright, in *Surprised by Hope*, puts it well:

> With Easter, God's new creation is launched upon a surprised world, pointing ahead to the rebirth of the entire creation. Every act of love, every work of true creativity – doing justice, making peace, healing families, is an earthly event in a long history of things that *implement* Jesus's own resurrection and *anticipate* the final new creation and act as signposts of hope.

We must abandon our small images of the divine. Our hope lies in the real God who leads from the front and is busy drawing all safely home. Jesus emphasises this divine drawing when he says:

*'No one – we might say 'no thing' – can come to me without the drawing of the Father'.*

(Jn 6:44, 55)

God is orchestrating all the dynamics of Creation and so can achieve its intended destination.

# 6: THE COSMOS IS ALREADY BEING DIVINISED

The divinisation of humankind was a central source of hope and joy in the Early Church. It retained its importance among the Greeks but had faded from view in the Latin Church, except when a drop of water is added to the wine at the Offertory of Mass: '*may we come to share in the divinity of Christ, who humbled himself to share in our humanity*'. Happily in our time the paramount significance of divinisation is re-emerging, and its scope is seen to include creation itself. In a superb paragraph of *Laudato Si* we read:

'The Eucharist is an act of cosmic love which joins heaven and earth; it embraces and penetrates all creation. The world which came forth from God's hands returns to him in blessed and undivided adoration. In the bread of the Eucharist creation is projected towards divinisation, towards unification with the Creator himself.' (LS 236).

This breath-taking vision of a divinised world is the ultimate and unshakeable ground for Christian hope for our small blue planet. Because Jesus is one of us, because he is part of creation just as we are, every crumb of matter, down to the last speck, is touched by his divinity. He is the exemplar of human divinisation. His Incarnation reaches down into the furthest depths of our material world and transfigures them. While we are indeed made of dust –

though we now know it is stardust! – our deepest reality is that we are made in the image of God (Gen 1:27).

We have then the capacity to become like God, and God works continuously from within and outside us to achieve its completion. We can catch glimpses of what is going on, as happened for Thomas Merton when he was looking at the crowd in a shopping mall. He writes, 'I suddenly saw the secret beauty of their hearts, the core of their reality, the person that each one is in God's eyes'.

Our messy lives are in fact a love story, a love affair between God, ourselves and creation. Since love makes like, 'we shall become like the Lord, because we shall see him as he is' (1 Jn 3:2). God becomes human so that humans may become divine. The making of us into divine images will be achieved as we enter into eternal life.

No matter how the history of our planet unfolds in the short term, the final and definitive shaping of the cosmos is in good hands. The Second Vatican Council's hope-filled message for humankind still holds true:

'We do not know the moment of the consummation of the earth and of humankind, nor the way the universe will be transformed. God is preparing a new dwelling and a new earth whose happiness will surpass all the desires for peace which arise in human hearts. Then death will have been conquered, the daughters and sons of God will be raised in Christ, the works of charity will remain and all of creation will be set free. Here on earth the kingdom is mysteriously present: when the Lord comes it will enter into its perfection' (*The Church in the Modern World*, 39).

# 7: May Nothing be Lost!

'Gather up the fragments lest any be lost' (Jn 6:12). This was Jesus' command to the disciples after the feeding of the 5,000 in the desert, and they filled twelve baskets with the crumbs that lay around! Can we relate this image to the Creation Story? We worry about the future of Earth, which as we know is finite and will eventually become a lifeless planet due to the heat generated by our exploding sun. But this limitedness can free us to think in a new way about the future planned for Creation by God. Can we allow ourselves to believe that this future will not be simply intra-historical but that it is already taking shape in a higher dimension?

Christian belief is that the dead are already being raised to this higher dimension: St Paul speaks of Jesus as the first-fruits of the resurrection, and that the full harvest is already being gathered in. '*What is sown is perishable, but what is raised is imperishable*' (see 1 Cor 15:20–58). And what in fact is raised? Surely we don't rise as ghosts, empty-handed: surely, like the risen Lord in the Gospel accounts, we will be fully alive! All the good we did on Earth will go with us (Rev 14:13), and we will rise as our full selves, in our inimitability and uniqueness, and with our particular styles, affections, relationships, emotions, thoughts, memories and experiences. All these are what make us what we are as unique images of God, and surely all that is love-tinged of them will accompany us into eternal life. What is not good will be cleansed and healed: our '*spots and wrinkles*' will be smoothed out '*so that we may be holy and without blemish*' (Eph 5:27). May we not hope that those who have already died are now sharing their stories, deepening their love of one another, exploring joyfully the details of the weaves of divine providence that has brought them together?

'*Bring what you have caught*' said Jesus as he prepared breakfast for the hungry disciples on the lake-shore. We have so much to bring, because perhaps nothing is 'lost and gone forever'. The death of those we love or of a species that took millions of years to reach its present form, the passing of natural beauty – all such things rightly grieve us, but they will be restored to us.

In one of his most moving poems, 'The Leaden Echo and the Golden Echo', Hopkins invites us to 'give beauty back to God, beauty's self and beauty's giver', because all that we forfeit is kept for us with a fonder care than we could have kept it.

C S Lewis suggests that memory may have a central role in all of this: that through it we can re-create and share what we now think of as past. All love and beauty, all the joys of life, will be refreshed and made new: the fields of our childhood – long ago built on – will be there in the fullness of their reality to enchant us. To God all things are present, and once our time boundaries melt away, what was past will be present again. So may it be that all that was worthwhile, beautiful and meaningful to us will be there again for our shared enjoyment – and of course let this include our pets and all the captivating wonders of Nature!

The prisoners in Plato's cave-myth (*Republic*, Book VII) could see only shadows, but the one who escaped suddenly saw everything in its true colour, form and harmony. Like those prisoners we often find life burdensome. We live in the shadow of the Paschal Mystery: we find ourselves laboring in the foreboding of Holy Thursday, in the agony of Good Friday, in the dark emptiness of Holy Saturday. All too rarely we find ourselves bathed in the glory of Easter Sunday, but may it be that the culminating episode in the endlessly amazing story of our small blue planet lies here, in '*the restoration of all things*' (Acts 3:21), when once again God will survey all that has been made, pronounce it '*very good*' (Gen 1:31) and present it to us for our eternal enjoyment?

# Sources

Attenborough, David: TV series

Bruteau, B: *The Grand Option,* 2001

Cannato, J: *Radical Amazement,* 2006
Cox, Brian: TV series
Cronin, M: *Irish and Ecology,* 2019
CSJ Ministry of the Arts: *Once Upon a Universe in Story &
    Song,* 2008

Dawkins, R: The God Delusion, 2006
De Chardin, T: Writings

Feehan, J: *God in a Five-pointed Star: A Spiritual Philosophy
    of Nature,* 2018
Fox, M: Writings

Harari, YN: *Sapiens: A Brief History of Humankind,* 2011
Harari, YN: *Homo Deus: A Brief History of Tomorrow*, 2016

Johnson, E: *Ask the Beasts, 2014; Creation and the Cross,*
    2018

Leon-Dufour, X: *Dictionary of Biblical Theology,* 1988
Lewis, C S: *Mere Christianity,* 1952; *Letters to Malcom*,
    1964.
Lonergan, B: *Insight,* 1957

McLaughlin, N: *Life's Delicate Balance,* 2016

*National Geographic*

Pope Francis: *Laudato Si,* 2015

Rovelli, C: *Seven Brief Lessons on Physics,* 2014
Rovelli, C: *Reality is Not What It Seems,* 2016

Schonborn, C: *Happiness, God and Man,* 2010
*Scientific American*
Swimme, B and Berry, T: *The Universe Story,* 1992

Thunberg, G: *No One is Too Small to Make a Difference,* 2019

Wallace-Wells, D: *The Uninhabitable Earth,* 2019
Wohlleben, P: *The Hidden Life of Trees,* 2016
Wright, N T: *Surprised by Hope,* 2007

… and many others.

Note that in this booklet scriptural quotations are sometimes abbreviated or adapted for reasons of space. For the same reason references are not given: every item of information has its own source. Most material is in the public domain. The Internet provides immense data – sometimes conflicting – on every topic touched on. All details given are open to correction; amendment will be gratefully received.

# NOTES

# NOTES